THE CENTER *of* ME

THE JOURNEY TO FINDING YOUR INNER COACH

LAURA L. BARRY

Bulk quantities are available for purchase: www.laurabarry.org

Copy-Editing: Margaret Diehl
Cover Design and Layout: Genevieve Glassy, Gorham Printing
Sketch Artist: Lisa Cicalese McMillen, Cica Lisa Designs

First Edition: March, 2015
Printed in the United States of America
ISBN: 978-0-9861471-0-4

This book is dedicated to my parents,
Marie and Jerry,
who taught me what fear and love look like,
and to my beautiful sons,
Thomas and Eric,
may you always know, nurture and talk
with your inner coach.

Contents

INTRODUCTION

This book has mostly written itself. It comes from the spiritual deep unknown. The examples I've used are real. I created the *"Try This"* suggestions for loving ways to support you on this journey. (Make sure your breaths are full deep belly, chest expanding breaths!)

There is an opportunity for deep spiritual work if you are willing. It is my hope that you and a "co-spiriteur" (friend, spouse or loved one) will read this book together. There is strength in numbers. (Remember, when two or more are gathered...) When doing the *"Try This"* parts, be open and honest with one another and repeat the exercises as often as needed until you feel you are coming from a place of authenticity. Share your insights and newly gained self-awareness with one another.

You will know you are authentic because you will not be looking for validation from the other in your sharing. You will share who you are because you no longer can hide your greatness... even if you think it still has a few gnarls. Gnarls give character and depth and make any wood floor or table most beautiful!

Thank you for taking the time to nurture yourself and feed your soul. It doesn't matter why you've picked up this book, just that you did.

May we love like Jesus, Buddha, Dalai Lama, Anthony DeMello, Desmond Tutu, Rumi, Mother Teresa, Amma, Pope Francis and all the others whose inner voice (regardless of any struggle) chooses love.

Bless you on your journey,

Laura

CHAPTER ONE

INSIDE

VOICES

We seem to have many internal voices providing us guidance: coach, critic, ego, spirit, intuition. These really boil down to only two, the fearful voice and the loving voice.

The fear voice is usually the one to speak first, possibly a bit louder and definitely longer. It's the one that holds you back, keeps you down, and wants you to stay stuck. Fear keeps you living in "wanting." It is my best critic. Fear says "Stick with me, I'll keep you safe."

The loving voice on the other hand, is your coach. It is much softer yet in complete support of you. It encourages you to move through intention into action. Love says, "You *already are* safe."

So, how do I tame and train this fear voice? As with anything in our lives, once there is awareness, change can begin.

I think about my children and the encouraging words I gave and continue to give to them. I think about the coaches they've had, the ones who have pushed them, helped them grow, succeed and excel. As a parent I loved these wonderful influences in their lives. These coaches were good, and they were tough; they coached with a higher level of awareness.

They've also had their share of coaches who mostly criticized, who blindly coached "the way they were coached." I remember watching my son Eric play baseball in elementary school. This was a turning point for me. Ultimately, Eric developed such a fear he decided to drop out. His coach meant well; however, he could only coach in the derogatory, verbally belittling way he was coached. It was unproductive to many of the young athletes. Eric's shoulders would rise in stress and anxiety every time he got to bat. My heart went out to him.

I don't know what the voice in Eric's head said to him. I only know what my voice said to him.

And, right then and there, I received a gift.

The gift of my awareness that as I supported others, as I encouraged my children, as I spoke confidence into *their* minds, so too, I needed to do this for me! We all need to do this for ourselves. I must be my own coach, cheerleader and confidant. The world will supply me with critics.

And so the journey continues.

THE AIRPORT TEST

Imagine you have to be stuck at an airport for seven or eight hours.

Quickly choose five people (ones you personally know and are alive, not celebrities or fantasies) whom you'd like to have there with you. (Not that you are really wishing an airport delay on yourself or anyone.)

1. ....

2. ....

3. ....

4. ....

5. ....

WHY? Why is it that these are the folks you chose? Most likely it's because these people are enjoyable to be around… maybe fun or funny, interesting, light-hearted, genuinely nice, caring and most likely good-humored. I've yet to come across anyone who chooses to be stuck with someone who is negative, always criticizing, skilled at finding fault or just unpleasant.

That seems to make so much sense. We wouldn't choose to be around or in a situation that brings us down, let alone one that makes a bad situation worse. When we dislike something that is happening around us the last thing we want or need is more complaining or criticizing – we don't need to add fuel to the fire.

The truth is even though we *say* we want positive things around us, we fill our lives every day with the negative. Whether it's the news we watch, some of our friends, our coworkers or clients, music, or the Facebook posts we read, we continually surround ourselves with information and people who fall into this group. They're somewhere on the scale between having a bad day and toxic.

I understand that sometimes there are situations we are not able to easily change. Family falls into this category. Coworkers and clients may as well. So instead of focusing on the situations not yet easily changeable, let's start with something powerful that we *can* change and, importantly, when aware, can control.

This is the most important of all! Yes, there is one significant, all-encompassing, never-separate-from-us entity that influences our every action, experience and attitude. It is the voice inside our head. (If you just said to yourself "what voice?" that is the voice!)

This voice, our voice, can either be a critic or a coach. Probably, you've experienced both sides of this voice. Most likely the critic drowns out the coach. We listen to this voice all day. Its nonstop chatter influences our very being. It has an opinion on everything. If we consciously paid attention to it, we would be exhausted – if it were someone outside of us, we would want him or her to shut up. We'd cry "uncle."

Yet we don't.

This nonstop chatter just goes on and on and on. It says things like: not good enough, not rich enough, not thin enough, not happy enough, not fast enough, not tall enough, not good looking enough, not . . . . enough. (You fill in the blank.) It's all about what we're *not*; it points out a made-up lack. It will tell you: you'll never be . . . . , or never have . . . . and can't do . . . .

If someone else continually criticized us like this, that person would never make our airport list! Why then would we allow ourselves to talk to us like that? Why would we choose to listen to that all day?

Maybe we've not been aware of this happening or how often it happens. Possibly we think it is normal. And even though it may be "normal" for you, it is not healthy! Once we recognize that we have this negative self-talk, we can never go back and feign unawareness. It's like once we realize putting our hand on a hot stove will burn and hurt, we cannot undo that awareness. We now have the choice to hurt or not hurt ourselves in that manner. Likewise, we now have the choice of how we silently speak to ourselves.

Most likely we do not realize it is a choice. It's just out of habit that we do this. As with any habit, we have the ability to make a change. We can break the habit. The definition of a habit is a settled or regular activity – something we do over and over again. And every time we practice our habit, we reinforce it. The first step in breaking any habit is just the awareness, the recognition, that we have it at all. The second step is finding the willingness to do it differently.

Given that a habit is a regular practice, we want to at least make this negative self-talk irregular, until eventually nonexistent. Later in the book we will get into strategies and specific tactics to help with this shift away from the **practice** of negative self-talk to a **practice** of positive self-talk. I'll go a step further and not even call it "positive" self-talk, because it is more than that. The energy it carries needs to come from a place of authenticity and sincerity. Instead, I'll refer to it as the voice of a friend or a loving self-talk. Let's talk to ourselves the way we would speak to our best friend.

COACH OR CRITIC

I am fond of words, and the dictionary is by far my favorite book. (Even though I use my MacBook dictionary most of the time, I still have several old hardbound dictionaries.)

To make sure we are on the same page, let's define critic and coach.

According to my MacBook dictionary, a critic is a person who expresses an unfavorable opinion of something. In the same sourced thesaurus, synonyms to critic are: attacker, faultfinder, back-seat driver and (now my favorite) gadfly.

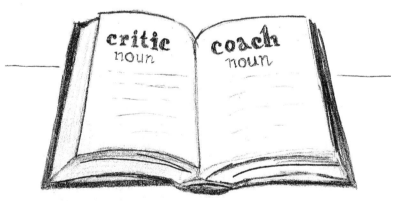

Likewise, a coach is someone who prompts or teaches and the synonyms are "trainer," "mentor," and "guru." I would add "supporter," "trusted adviser," one who is both honest and encouraging for me to be a better me… someone who will cheer me on to do my best. When I think about the coaches in my life, they have all been someone who knew better than I what I was capable of accomplishing, and they pushed me. They provided me with the tools I needed so I could experience greater success.

While both a critic and coach are aware of possible weaknesses, the critic stays stuck and focuses on the negative. The coach provides solutions and encouragement. One focuses on lack or fault and the other on the potential, the possibilities.

Hmmm…. Given these definitions, whom would I choose to have by my side? On whose guidance and advice would I choose to rely? Since the critic's only interest is in blame, fault, lack and attack, I would choose the coach any day. Yet my thoughts may indicate I choose the critic.

The critic voice interferes with compassion, kindness, self-love and personal growth. It is disruptive to our self-supporting success because it knows no boundaries, doesn't wait to be asked its opinion and certainly could not care less about the impact it has as long as it remains in power. It is unfeeling and ruthless. It leaves one with numerous feelings of being less than and powerless.

The coach voice is experienced, sensitive and far subtler than the critic voice. It is always there, yet waits to be called upon. It requires awareness and willingness to be triggered. It's like a muscle that hasn't been used much – it doesn't take a lot to get great results.

HACKING

We all have a heightened sensitivity to computers being hacked and the possibility that our personal information can be made available to the general public. What if our thoughts could be hacked? What if our thoughts could be exposed to the outside world? Often we spend more time and energy covering up how we really feel about ourselves than doing anything to change our thoughts. This is exhausting.

When my children were little, once in a while I would hear them say a self-derogatory thought out loud. It might have been something as simple as "I'm so stupid" – and I would respond, "Don't you ever let me hear you talk about my son that way, you hear me? You'll be in BIG trouble because my son is NOT stupid! He is bright and witty and loved!"

It would bring a smile to his gorgeous face, and importantly, it would interrupt the negative thoughts. I could help him catch himself before his mood spiraled down and made a tough situation worse. And sometimes my admonition would lead to a conversation about what was really going on.

Wouldn't it be nice to have someone interrupt us when we got on this negative track? Let's face it, if we could pop a pill and have our negative self-talk go away, we would. The remedy however doesn't come in pill form, nor can it come from someone else if our thoughts haven't been hacked. It's an inside job.

It actually takes less energy – and is more rewarding – to pay attention to our thoughts and question them than it does to pretend that everything is okay. Imagine doing this with a physical injury. We wouldn't think of hiding a broken bone or a deep laceration – no, we would seek help to get it fixed. Yet we injure ourselves with thoughts all the time and pretend they are not there.

Pretend – or "make believe" as I would call it as a child – is to play a made-up, invented part. It requires us to let go of the truth and don a false front. This might be fun on Halloween, but exhausting to do every day.

Sit quietly, relax and take in three deep breaths through your nose. Close your eyes and hold yourself in a loving space. Let yourself know you want to come from a place of compassion. Take a few moments to completely relax. Envision your thoughts, your brain, getting hacked. What would you like to have come out? What negative words would you like to have removed forever? List them:

Even if you don't really believe it at this point, what kind words about you would you like to have exposed? These are words you would like to be said about you. What are these words?

Once you've written these things, release each of these negative words saying:

I release my thought of ....

about myself, and replace it with ....

(use one of the kind words).

Finally, dig a little deeper and ask what would you like others to know about you. Maybe you are very sensitive, and that's why you pretend nothing bothers you.... Maybe you are lonely, and that is why you keep so busy.... Maybe you are scared, and that is why you seem to not accomplish the great things others know you can. Be honest.

Take a few minutes to write down these thoughts:

Then close your eyes again and thank yourself for being honest and loving. Thank yourself for allowing your thoughts to be hacked so you can see yourself with loving eyes.

If you are not reading the book with a co-spiriteur, is there someone in your life with whom you could share this? If you are reading this book with a co-spiriteur, or have someone with whom to share, perhaps you can lovingly talk together about your thoughts being hacked. Sometimes the scariest thing is to tell another our deepest, most intimate thoughts about ourselves. We think if they only knew .... about me they would never be my friend. Maybe... Maybe not. Maybe it would actually deepen your relationship.

When you are sharing, be gentle with each other. Don't dismiss the other's feelings by saying things like: "How can you say that?" or "That's ridiculous, you're not that way" or "I can't believe you feel that way about yourself." Truly listen to each other and gently explore each other's feelings. Maybe ask, "When did you first start feeling that way?" or "Would you like to know how I see you?" If you are the listener, ask permission to provide input. Don't assume you are welcome to give advice or commentary.

Wouldn't it be nice to have an authentic relationship versus one based on your hiding your true self? We may be able to deceive others for a while, but we cannot deceive ourselves. It will ooze out of us in one self-loathing or sabotaging way or another. I'd rather be disliked for who I am than liked for who I'm not. I don't have the desire or energy for pretense. And doesn't it take a LOT of energy to hide and pretend?

When we tiptoe into being authentic about ourselves with another, there is a certain vulnerability about it. How we expose our inner selves with another can feel risky, and we may feel fear. This is also true when we become vulnerable with just ourselves. When we peel away at the layers that we've been hiding under, it can be a bit scary. But how else can our light shine through if we are unable (or unwilling) to peel away that which is hiding our light?

We think we are afraid of the unknown. That is not true. If it were truly unknown, there could be no fear. We are afraid of what we tell ourselves about the unknown. It is our thoughts that create the fear. We subconsciously create a story about the unknown, making it a known, and then react to that story. We project our unquestioned story into the future and then behave as though it were true. If it were truly unknown, there would be nothingness. And certainly nothing to fear.

The unknown is not to be feared. Our version of it, the story we tell ourselves about it, is what we fear.

So I say, hack away! Shed light on your thoughts, expose them for what they are… just unquestioned thoughts. Bringing them out in the open doesn't make them any more or less real, and might actually reveal how unfounded they are.

WHOSE VOICE IS IN THERE?

This sounds like a funny question – if it's my head, it must be my voice. But hold on there, not so quickly… maybe the voice inside your head is an old tape playing the voice of a teacher who did not have confidence in you and told you that you couldn't cut it, or of a parent who possibly belittled you or told you you'd never amount to anything. Maybe it's the school bully's voice, or that of a boss or coworker. Are there feelings or inadequacies that seem to have always been there? Clearly, the possibilities of whose voice is in your head are endless. It just takes one time being made fun of, being put down or hearing hurtful words… *one time*, and then *we* perpetuate that thought over and over again. We take over the attack on ourselves without even realizing it.

Perhaps it will help to get to the root cause of your beliefs, I don't know. Sometimes with this type of investigation, we tend to go back, assign blame and stay stuck in what happened "to me." Some forms of modern therapy allow this. You uncover what a parent did or did not do that is the cause of why you are how you are, and then you get to blame. Whew… we are relieved it is not our fault. Someone else is to blame for my behavior and thoughts and unhappiness. Damn that person… how horrible all this is, woe is me, blah, blah, blah.

That is *not* the intent! The intent is to become aware of our current belief system and with gentleness realize that we are the ones keeping the past negative, hurtful thoughts alive. We are the ones doing this to ourselves. There is no more "someone else." There is no more blame. Maybe someone pointed us in the wrong thought direction; however, we can choose to get off that path. No one is holding us hostage on that path any longer but ourselves.

Let me give a personal example. When my children were in elementary school, there was a school holiday bazaar for which I volunteered. Specifically, I volunteered to help set up.

Now, as background, you need to know the story I tell myself is that I do not have a creative bone in my body. I want to; it is not for a lack of trying. And in all honesty, I am very creative in fashion and culinary endeavors.

Years ago, when I was just out of college, I decided to make a wreath for my new apartment door. It took me weeks to make this thing. I even had to go to a craft store, a first for me. I was so proud of myself. I thought it was so beautiful. I hung the wreath on the door, and I had a date for the next night. I knew that this wreath would be very impressive to my date! No doubt about it, very impressive. My date showed up, and as we were leaving my apartment and I closed the door, I said to him, "Do you like my wreath?" And he replied politely with a simple yes. Clearly he was not getting the significance of the wreath. I told him I made it, because that would surely open his eyes, and he would be very impressed. He smiled and responded, "You did?" Now we were getting somewhere. Now he realized what a catch I was! And I said proudly, "Yes, I made this wreath!" He paused for a moment and his response was, "Really? What grade were you in?"

He thought I had saved the wreath from my childhood… In actuality, I *was* still a student. I was in grad school. I laughed then, and I still laugh now when I think of this story.

Back to the bazaar. My thought about just setting up was that I did not have a creative bone in my body, but I could help people bring their things in, put up tables, organize chairs, work in the kitchen and help clean up to get ready for the two-day event. When I got there, the Chair of this event, Mary, said to me, "Oh, Laura, I'm so glad you're here early. You are so creative, could you please organize the tables and start to place all of the crafts on them and make them look good?" She wanted *me* to organize and creatively place the crafts on the display tables. Clearly, she had not heard my wreath story.

But guess what? I did it. For three years, I was known as the one who would organize the tables because of how creatively and beautifully I could do it. I still chuckle at this, but I remember at the time thinking Mary doesn't know, so I'll play along with it! In all actuality, I'm the one that didn't know. I'm the one who got a shift in perception and undid old belief systems. An old belief system I created! Okay, I may not be the best wreath maker, but that doesn't mean I am not creative in other ways.

With childlike curiosity ask yourself why you'd choose to stay on this path with someone else's voice and cement these things in your mind? Why would you repeat these things about yourself? Are you willing to challenge what someone said? Ask if your thoughts are serving you now for your highest good? Placing blame gives your internal gadfly (my new favorite synonym for critic) way too much power. It fuels the fire of anger and does little to support the internal shift from critic to coach and cheerleader.

It starts with awareness that this is even happening! I prefer to understand what is happening in the present and to challenge the present thought. We all have a set of beliefs about ourselves. These come from years of accepting either what others have said about us, or thoughts that we've had about ourselves. It stems from insecurities and a belief that we are less than. Many religions teach us this as well… that we are not worthy. The key is not necessarily from where these beliefs came, but rather *why* do we hold on to them? Why do we hold on to something that limits us? Something that is negative? That is not empowering? Is it serving a purpose? It has to serve a purpose. Does it give you an excuse as to why you are not successful? Healthy? Kind? Happy? Is it someone else's fault you are lonely, overweight or miserable? Is that the reason there is self-sabotage in your life? Regardless of the purpose, it sure does keep you stuck!

The question is, are you replaying someone else's opinion inside your head? Is someone else's voice taking up prime real estate in your thoughts? Importantly, are you ready to let go of these thoughts through awareness that they are there, inquiry around how these thoughts limit you, gentleness in dealing with the new emotions and thoughts that may arise, and, most importantly, shift to self-love and self-appreciation?

The last I heard, a statue has never been erected to a critic!

Sit quietly, relax and take in three deep breaths through your nose. Close your eyes and hold yourself in a loving space. Let yourself know you want to come from a place of compassion. Take a few moments to completely relax. Think of a belief you have about yourself that you would like to stop nurturing.

I'll never be ....

or I can't ....

(It is important to use your words.)

Do you know how this thought first entered your belief system? Gently tell yourself you are really sorry for continuing to repeat this to you. Using compassion, lovingly hold yourself... perhaps literally hug yourself or hold your hand. Let yourself know that you realize it doesn't make you feel good. The words hurt. Tell yourself you want to be your own best friend. You want to stop saying these things – you will stop saying these things. Then ask yourself for loving and compassionate support as you change this pattern of behavior. Tell yourself that you love yourself. Make up a new saying in place of the old one and say it three times. Thank yourself for being loving and supportive during this talk. Then, when ready, take three more breaths through the nose and open your eyes.

This exercise is to be done slowly. You may even have a trusted friend do this with you, someone who can read one sentence to you at a time – with perhaps a minute in between each one. Or consider taping your own voice and replaying it to yourself.

What was the new saying?

Take a moment to write how this process felt and how you feel about your new saying:

How do you want to show love to yourself?

....
....
....
....

What words can you use to show yourself love?

....
....
....
....

It may feel uncomfortable at first to "be talking to yourself" like this. And herein lies the irony! We can talk negatively all day to ourselves about ourselves, and while we may not like it, it is comfortable. This nasty self-talk is what should be uncomfortable! Saying "You Rock!" "You're the best!" and "Man, I love you!" to yourself ought to be what is comfortable.

The goal here is to have loving and caring self-talk be equally as comfortable as the negative self-talk until one day the complete reverse happens.... One day, the positive, loving self-talk will be comfortable, and the negative, self-demoting talk will be uncomfortable! How's that for a goal?

 Try This •

Every morning upon awakening, state your new saying to yourself three times. Repeat this again before going to sleep. If so inclined, write this out on a card and keep with you as a reminder to say it throughout the day.

THE EXCEPTION TO THE COACH/CRITIC RULE

Okay, it's not really a rule; however, there may come a time when you think that a critic can inspire and motivate someone to be the best that they can be. However, being motivated by something negative still creates angst and unsettledness, plants seeds of negativity and doubt even though the outcome may be a good one. Any time we use fear to motivate us, there are consequences.

A perfect example of this is my sister, Maureen. Maureen was a hard worker in school yet good grades did not come easily to her, and she studied diligently. She was in the robust nursing program at Villanova University, and even prior to being admitted, the dean of her program told her and my father during a campus visit that Maureen would not be successful, as she thought Maureen's background and grades were academically weak.

After much discussion, the dean was willing to give Maureen a chance and accepted her for that first semester, but only on academic probation.

Well, Maureen was an accomplished athlete. She was used to opponents "bad-talking" to weaken confidence. She didn't succumb to this from an opponent on the court, nor would she from this dean, although it planted a seed of doubt she would spend the next four+ years overcoming.

Fast-forward the four college years. Maureen graduated with honors, was in the nursing honor society, and was chosen by the class to give the graduation address to the nursing students. When the ceremony was over, with diploma in hand and nursing cap on head, she visited this dean. They spoke for a while, and the dean responded, "I'm glad you proved me wrong."

Maureen was thrilled to be able to prove the dean wrong. However, how much more successful might Maureen have been if she had had an advocate? How much less stress, angst and doubt might she have experienced if the dean had believed in her, been a coach, a resource, a mentor? Well, we will never know. What I do know is that this seed of doubt stayed with Maureen while she got her Masters and other advanced degrees in nursing, including Adult Nurse Practitioner.

This seed weakened her confidence and took years to "outgrow." So, even with her ultimate successes, what she was told early on carried through. The outcome may have been great. The end doesn't always justify the means.

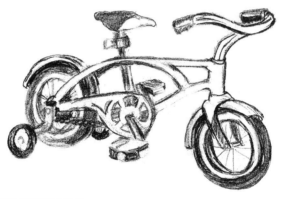

TRAINING WHEELS

I worked in hospice for a couple of years, and a frequent discussion both patients and families had with me concerned how they wished they had done things differently. Reviewing one's life is common in hospice. The dying person looks back and often wishes things had been different and questions why they behaved the way they did. Families of the patient also revisit the past and are upset with themselves for not visiting more, for the fights they had. They wish it had been different.

The sad truth is, like those facing the end of earthly life, (I say *earthly* because my belief is that although the vessel that is housing this life [the body] is no longer needed or necessary, life still exists. The source of life that was in our body now lives without being tethered by the body.), many of us use our current wisdom to go back and analyze a situation and wish we had acted in a different way. This can result in regret, disappointment, anger or shame. This puts our negative self-talk on steroids.

Let me repeat that one key sentence again: we use our *current* wisdom to go back and analyze a situation and then wish we had acted differently! We don't use the wisdom we had at the time of the event for which we are beating ourselves up about – no, we use our current wisdom. The issue with this is that we have greater wisdom today than we did yesterday, last week, last year or many years ago. So, in one sense, it is ridiculous to do this. Twenty years ago, we couldn't text someone. Why would I waste energy wishing I had been able to text? Why would we fret over not doing something in the past that was impossible to do in the past? Yet we do. And believe it or not, next year we will look back on today and see how much we've grown.

Remember when you first started to ride a two-wheeler bicycle and needed training wheels? What if we used our current wisdom to go back and evaluate our five-year-old self? Our current self probably knows how to ride a two-wheeler. Would we beat ourselves up for not knowing how to ride a two-wheeler when we were five years old? Would we say, "Oh, how stupid I must've looked" or "I can't believe my muscles weren't strong enough, you dumb weakling" or "Those training wheels were so embarrassing?" Probably not. (Hopefully not.) Why? Because we know we did the best we could, and we were learning to become better. And, it really seems silly to beat ourselves up over something in the past that we know we can do differently now.

I saw this sign the other day: "I never beat myself up gently." Using *gently* to describe *beat up* is an oxymoron. This is a sad and probably too familiar feeling. Let's get rid of the word *gently.* "I never beat myself up!" But how? Where to begin?

In Western culture, especially in America, this "using current wisdom to evaluate the past and then beat ourselves up" is a common thing. Did you know that in the Buddhist philosophy this would not occur? In Buddhism, when a person reflects on something from the past and realizes, using current wisdom, that she could do it differently now, she celebrates that she has learned, that she has grown; and she is excited to have this new wisdom!

She celebrates, not beats herself up. How delicious is that?

Can you see the critic/coach difference? The critic is stuck on beating up; the coach (Buddhist way) sees and is grateful for the learning. The critic is imprisoned by her thoughts and her negativity. The coach has grown in learning and awareness and can now move forward in the world with kinder ways.

If we look at life as a classroom, then everything is a lesson. When occurrences are lessons, we get to practice over and over until we are accomplished and ready to move up a grade. One day we won't need the training wheels. Until we are ready to take them off, however, they serve a purpose.

Try This

Sit quietly, relax and take in three deep breaths through your nose. Close your eyes and hold yourself in a loving space. Let yourself know you want to come from a place of compassion. Take a few moments to completely relax. What past situation do you replay over and over and beat yourself up over? Can you remember how you felt at the time of the event(s)? Were you scared? Lonely? Ashamed? Can you see that you did the best you could with the skills and knowledge you had? Are you willing to forgive yourself for thinking you could have done it differently? Are you willing to forgive yourself for making you relive this event over and over again? Can you have compassion for this younger you? Are you willing to be the loving coach to this younger you? Thank your younger you for doing the best that s/he could. Say you are sorry for not remembering and realizing how really hard it was back then. Ask for forgiveness from your younger self. Make a promise that you will look at this differently, more gently in the future.

Thank yourself for the lessons you learned in this.

Now, take a few moments and write a love note to your younger self.
(Use more paper if needed.)

Was there resistance to this exercise? If so, no judgment! Just notice you have resistance. Resistance is a form of fear. It is a shrewd way to keep one stuck. It is sneaky and makes you feel justified in staying stuck.

CHAPTER TWO

OUTSIDE

THE SOLES OF OUR FEET

Our thoughts are not limited to just ourselves about ourselves. Our thoughts extend outward as well. This is why it is critical to clean up our inner talk. If we trash self-talk, we just trash-talk. It is hard to separate out our levels of negativity. There is not a continuum between good/bad mental talk and right/wrong thinking; each thought is loving, or it isn't. Trash-talk goes beyond what we say about ourselves; it expands into what we say and think about others, how we judge others and how we view the world around us. Our outer world is a reflection of what's going on inside of us and what our thoughts are.

Ever notice how we always know how others should behave? When we are uncomfortable, usually the first thing we do is judge how "they" should behave differently. We notice this because it is a way for us to feel better, possibly superior. We want things outside of us to change in lieu of changing the inside of us. Trust me, I'm an expert at this. I know how everyone else should live, act, vote, dress, eat, etc., to make me feel comfortable. If everyone else would just do and be as I wanted, the world (my world) would be a better place. The trouble with this though is that you, along with everyone else, are probably thinking the same thing.

Anytime you need the external world to change for your happiness, that's an opportunity for you to dig deeper. It's a chance to check in with your internal voice and see what thoughts are percolating, what judgments you're making. Any voice and any thoughts that do not result in joy and peace within you are up for review. As we start to pay attention to our inner voice, we realize that we are judgmental; we pre-judge; we have internal thoughts that make us uneasy; and quite frankly we would prefer to change the outside versus the inside.

There is an analogy in Buddhism about this external/internal change: (Paraphrased) if you are barefoot, rather than covering up the whole surface of the earth with leather for your feet to be comfortable, you can just cover up the soles of your feet.

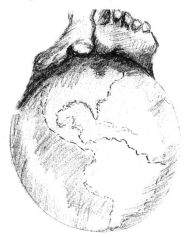

This means we need to address ourselves as individuals. Once we do this, the rest of the world feels like it is covered in leather. By taking care of ourselves, we are, in fact, making the world a more comfortable place in which to live.

This unease, judgment or "right/wrong" thinking is ALWAYS an opportunity to investigate further. A favorite quote from Rumi is: "Yesterday I was clever, so I wanted to change the world. Today I am wise, so I am changing myself."

Basically, there are three things we can do with any thought or mindset that is not loving, not peaceful and considerate or of a coaching, supportive nature:

1) IGNORE IT!

Yes, that is a choice. We can pretend that everything is okay, and we don't feel the way that we feel. We can push away our feelings and not pay attention to the negativity, judgment or anger in our thoughts. This may appear to work for a while; however, the toxicity is building up. We can ignore the stressors in our life for only so long. Eventually, what happens is that we will have a reaction or outburst that is disproportionate to what is really going on.

Over time, the pressure builds up until it cannot be contained and then there will be an explosion. Let me give you an example.

Several years ago, while at a weekly team manager's meeting, one team member, Dana (not real name), seemed to be a little stressed. It was a heavy workload period for everyone, and we were doing our best to figure out schedules given the upcoming Christmas and New Year holidays. Within 30 minutes, Dana was argumentative, and within 45 minutes of the meeting she got very angry, said some things about the heavy workload, the lack of respect from management, being given too many things to do last minute. She said she was tired of it all and stormed out of the room.

I texted Dana and asked to meet her for lunch. A couple of hours later we met, and when I asked what was going on, she first told me "nothing" and complained about work. I agreed it was a stressful time. Then, I sat quietly and asked what else… eventually she told me a tale of personal things that had happened over the past nine months, including infidelity and possible divorce.

WHOA… Dana was not responding to the team meeting, let alone being fully present at the team meeting. Her pent-up anger, feelings of disrespect and being overwhelmed in her personal life surfaced on the professional side. The stressful work situation was only the last straw.

Dana's reaction in the meeting was disproportionate to what was happening at the meeting. She was on overload, trying to ignore and stuff down the many stressful, emotional events happening outside of work, and this caused an explosion.

Your situation may be entirely different. It could be as simple as running late for work because you hit the snooze button one too many times and then being nasty or impatient with the barista at your local coffee shop. You are annoyed with yourself, unwilling to look at why you always do this to yourself (run late) and then you take it out on someone else. It is disproportionate behavior for what is actually occurring. Ignoring the source of the "issue" (YOU run late) means the anger or distress will come out sooner or later, often in ways you regret.

Try This

Sit quietly, relax and take in three deep breaths through your nose. Close your eyes and hold yourself in a loving space. Let yourself know you want to come from a place of compassion. Then, think about a time you overreacted to a situation. One (or many) will come to mind. Dismiss any judgments that may surface about it. This is not a time for judgment; it is a time for healing. Just stay present to the situation. Are you willing to dig deeper and find out what was really going on? Can you answer these questions:

What was I really upset about?

What was really going on for me?

....
....
....
....
....
....
....
....
....

What thoughts were going through my mind?

....
....
....
....
....
....
....
....
....

Lovingly thank yourself for sharing these thoughts and for creating a safe place to explore.

Take a moment to write how it felt to get underneath your disproportionate reaction:

What have you learned about the consequences of ignoring your thoughts and feelings?

2) EXACERBATE IT!

This is the second of the three things we can do with our thoughts and feelings. Believe it or not, we can actually pay attention to our feelings and make them worse. We all have that friend(s) or co-worker whom we can call to discuss an issue, who will listen to our ranting, agree with us and add fuel to the fire. This person will listen to our story and give us more ammunition. He or she will validate us and help keep the story and heightened emotion well-fertilized.

It is interesting to note that we have friends who would never allow us to stay stuck in judgment or self-righteousness like this. They would tell it like it is and that is exactly why we would not think of calling them. No, for some reason we know precisely whom to call when we want to make a situation worse, when we want this venomous thought process to grow or when we want to feel validated in our negativity and anger.

Some of us get so good at this, we may not even need someone else to aggravate the situation. We are so gifted that we can do this all by ourselves. We replay the situation over and over in our mind, the "he said/she said." We think of things we could have said. We think of things we will say next time. We tell ourselves, "I can't believe she did this to me..." or "How dare he talk to me like that..." or worse, "I'll show them..." and then think of vindictive things to say or do.

Whether aggravating the situation with someone else or just by ourselves, we perpetuate the anger or dis-ease. Neither does anything to help. They both hinder the process of healing and compassion and keep us stuck. It may feel good for a moment, but that is temporary and comes at a very high price: our inner peace and overall well-being.

What we don't realize when we are in a state of heightened emotion is that, though we are upset, the other person may not be aware of the problem or may not know *how* upset we are. AND, of course, he or she may not even care. Even when we have calmed down about the situation, if it is brought back up again (either through the critic voice in our head, reminding us of how this person did or said something hurtful or from another reminding us), we can go from calm to aggravated in the snap of a finger. Holding on to this kind of toxicity only hurts us. Holding on and nurturing this venom inside of us does nothing to remedy the issue, let alone allow for healing. Someone once said this is like drinking poison and expecting the other person to get sick.

3) INVESTIGATE IT!

The third thing we can do is investigate it. Yes! Dig deeper. Check your thoughts. Are you reacting emotionally, or are you clear-headed? What thoughts came up that created your reaction? Was it that this shouldn't be happening? Was it that you disagree with the other person and therefore they have to be wrong?

If we take a step back from the situation, can we see it for what it is? Is it that we just don't like / care for / want what is happening? Is it that we refuse to change our view of the matter and yet require that the other change their view? That may sound silly, especially when we KNOW we are right about the situation, yes? (Ha-ha.)

A Course In Miracles suggests that all we need to have is a little willingness to see things differently. In order to do this and NOT simply ignore it, we need to uncover the why. Getting to the why supports our willingness to shift our perception. It is never done to blame or beat ourselves up, but rather to encourage a gentle, loving understanding that we do not have to be afraid of ourselves and certainly not of our thoughts. We do not need to fear uncovering our truth. We no longer have to hide from ourselves. We can be authentic. And once we start to do this, it becomes addictive because living in peace and authenticity creates inner happiness and joy, which is our natural state.

It is our unquestioned thoughts that will cause us suffering. Without investigating, our judgmental thoughts are what show up. We believe them and then react accordingly.

Think about a time when you were on the road and a speeding car seemed to come up out of nowhere and passed you unsafely. What's the first thing that came to mind? What a jerk. Oh, s/he thinks he's so cool driving like that. S/he could kill us all. Really, what a .... (insert your own form of bad mouthing.) Were you secretly hoping that there was a cop ahead? Maybe you speeded up too? Be honest here.

Now, I'm not condoning poor or unsafe driving habits by any means, but by investigating our thoughts we can learn how really ignorant we are. How do we know that driver is really a jerk? We don't. Why would I think that driver thinks they are cool driving like that? I don't know. Why would I speed up and be a risky driver too? What exactly was the thought that changed my state of being? One moment I was contentedly driving and the next moment I had uncomfortable to intense feelings, all because of something I told myself about what I was seeing.

What if the driver was rushing to the hospital to see his wife deliver their first baby? Would that thought change your reaction to the situation?

See, we create the reasoning behind things without any curiosity as to the truth or possible other interpretations, and then we react as though it is true. Now that you are aware of this, let's play with it.

Try This

As you go through your day, when thoughts pop up around situations, question your thoughts. Just get curious. See how many times you can catch yourself in a made-up thought that may or may not have anything to do with reality.

I played this game with my mom once. (She didn't know I was playing.) She was telling me a story about someone, believing that he had been wrong and ill-mannered in a situation. (I'll use the name Gary.) She got into some of the specifics about what Gary did and why he did this particular thing. She thought it was just horrible, saying, "Can you believe he would do such a thing...?" Although she was not involved in any way, she was annoyed and judgmental as she told the story.

This is how the conversation went:

ME: Mom, did Gary tell you that is why he did this?

MOM: What do you mean?

ME: Well, you just said that Gary did this thing, and you told me the reason why. I was wondering how you knew the reason. Did Gary tell you?

MOM: No, it just makes sense for that to be the reason.

ME: So you don't know for sure that is the reason?

MOM: Well, no, I guess not.

ME: Could there be another reason, like… (I named a few)

MOM: (thinking for a while) I guess… yes, possibly.

ME: So, instead of thinking something about Gary that you don't know for a fact, and which is not very kind and is annoying to you, why wouldn't you think of other possibilities instead?

AND, God Bless This Woman… She contemplated this for a while and said: Because I'm 80 years old. I've been like this all my life and I'm not changing now! (Gotta LOVE it!)

I have to admire her willingness to tiptoe into the game and the strength of her conviction that her unquestioned thoughts serve her well. I loved her pure honesty about it. I also loved that I could release my expectations that she would change her mind after our discussion and, importantly, that I didn't require her to change her opinion or outlook to suit me.

But you get the point. She had made up a story in her mind, never questioned it and reacted to it as if it were true.

Investigation of our thoughts is critical to get to a place of authenticity.

EVIDENCE

What we look for is what we see. I have a dear running friend, Pat. She is a technical writer. Her job is to figure out all the ways an instruction could be misinterpreted. Her job is to find the ambiguity, notice when details are too sparse or language too jargony – to determine where the pitfalls are and correct them before they have a chance to cause problems. It's the sort of job that stretches your mind in a very particular way. On a run one day she was telling me how she's starting to do some of this in her personal life. Prior to a trip she was planning to take, she started thinking about all the negative things that could happen … from insane traffic to backed-up security to missing the plane. She was a wreck by time the flight took off. If she focused on all that could go wrong, not only would she NOT have an enjoyable trip, she would probably drive herself nuts.

What we look for is what we see. If I look for the good in you, that is what I see. If I look at you as doing the best you can for who you are, I can have compassion toward you. This is not to minimize or ignore the fact that there are abusive or toxic people /relationships. Rather, this attitude allows you, with compassion, to see the other as doing the best they can AND to realize you have a choice. Maybe the choice is to be more loving, maybe it's to seek counseling, maybe it is to walk away. Sometimes there is good in good-bye.

When we are looking for evidence to support thinking poorly about another or ourselves, we are exacerbating the situation. We stay stuck and strengthen our habit of blaming and finger-pointing. We find evidence to support our pre-conceived ideas. When we look for the bad and the wrong, that is what we will find.

When we step out of the blame mode, we are empowered. When we see others as being perfect just as they are, we have a choice. A choice to stay in relationship or not. A choice to support ourselves or not. A choice.

The point is, once we are on the whole and holy path of listening to our inner spirit, looking for love and having compassion, we have less tolerance for that which is not loving and truthful. We have less desire to seek evidence of ugliness and hostility and judgment and a much greater desire to surround ourselves with support and tenderness and gratitude.

I know that I would want others to see me as doing my best, so why wouldn't I extend that same mindset and courtesy to another? Isn't that what the Golden Rule is all about: *treat others the way we want to be treated.* I'd want to be given the benefit of the doubt if I were cranky; I'd want to be seen as having good intentions and being a loving, kind person. It is interesting to note that every major religion or thought system has some form of the Golden Rule in its sacred writings. If I agree with this Golden Rule principle, then I will look for evidence to support another doing his or her best. I will seek evidence of kindness, goodness and love.

In my evidence search, I also need to get in touch with my expectations. Just because your best doesn't meet my expectation, doesn't mean you are not at your best. It means I need to challenge my preconceived ideas about your best. I need to check inside of me. An unfulfilled expectation has nothing to do with the other; it is completely inside my head and is the result of unquestioned thoughts.

Try This

Sit quietly, relax and take in three deep breaths through your nose. Close your eyes and hold yourself in a loving space. Let yourself know you want to come from a place of compassion and kindness. Think of today as a gift to you. Imagine there will be no other like it (there won't), that abundant kindness will be yours today in the simplest of ways. Promise yourself that you will look for evidence of kindness today. You may find that you start being kinder during this process. Just look for a smile, a thank you, or a door held open. Notice kindness. And, importantly, be the evidence of compassion and kindness for someone else today.

Throughout the day, pause and reflect on the kindness in your life. Offer up gratitude for this awareness. Write notes to yourself about the kindness (yours or others) of which you were aware. At the end of the day, review your kindness notes.

What did you get out of this exercise? Was it easy to remember to do?

Did you find that you were easily able to express gratitude for being aware of your and others' kindness? Why or why not?

And lastly, was there resistance? (a.k.a. fear)

STUCK IN THE PAST

I am a rower, a sweep rower. This means I row with one oar and with either three or seven other rowers and a coxswain. I enjoy this sport immensely, both as participant and spectator. This sport has helped me learn how to stay in the present. Each stroke in the boat is just that, one stroke. When it is over, each member of the team must go on to the next. Sometimes this is hard if we've made a mistake in our stroke... caught a crab, missed the water, rushed the slide, etc... However, we cannot waste any energy on the mistake. We acknowledge it and move on. The team depends on each member being present in the boat, not lingering in the past. To linger in the past means one's focus, strength, drive and determination are not used in the current stroke. Someone is rowing at less than peak performance. This could cost the crew its race.

We cannot be in the past and the present at the same time. One or the other will suffer. This is true of any sport. If you focus on the mistake, you are in the past and cannot play the game that is present. Every sport has this mental component. Great athletes are the ones who can overcome their inner critic.

It is important to note that this doesn't just apply to the one making the mistake – it applies to the others on the team as well. If I focus on the mistake I made, I am not in the now; I am not at my best. If I focus on another's mistake (which is much easier to do), I still am not present. My concentration is off, and therefore I'm not at my best. It's a lose-lose situation. Our inner critic is sneaky this way. Our inner critic can just as easily criticize me as another. In fact, perhaps with another making the mistake, a little ego righteousness can ice the critic cake. Call it inner voice or ego – it just wants to criticize, keeping you focused on and stuck in the past.

Being stuck in the past is not just a problem for athletes. It can affect us all. Every time we relive or rethink about a moment from the past, every time we judge a mistake just for the sake of reliving it, blaming others or ourselves – or worse, mentally beat ourselves up – we fuel this inner critic. Scientists say we do this so often that we actually create neurological ruts in our brain, and we have the power to change this.

Let's take a page out of Hollywood in terms of mistakes. When on a set, as the film begins to roll, there is a clapboard that indicates which *take* it is. We've seen this on movie reels. They state the name of the scene and then "take 1," or "take 13" or "take 103." It's not a mistake, it's a mis-take. They get to take it over! It's a DO-OVER!

When was the last time you shouted "DO OVER" when you did something that, based on the outcome, you wished you'd had done differently? Really, please email me and tell me how old you were. I'm thinking I was six? Seven? Life is our classroom; we get DO OVERS all the time. With life as our classroom, we are *learning* all the time. And some lessons are just harder or more life-changing than others, agree?

Now, this is not to say that we are not responsible for our actions. We need to take full responsibility and be held accountable. But we don't have to beat ourselves up. Beating myself up keeps me stuck. Apologizing and feeling remorseful or sad allows me to honor the mis-take, perhaps make amends and, importantly, learn from it. If we stay stuck, we are not able to get to a place of healing. Staying stuck allows me to place blame and look externally for the cause of the suffering. If I made the mis-take, I am the cause of the suffering. I get to own up to that. Acknowledging my mis-take allows me to correct the situation as best I can, love myself for the aware-ness, and move on (no staying stuck!). Using this mis-take as a lesson, I now know one – or 10 – ways of not doing it anymore. And so, I try again, take # ....

If you stay stuck in the past, you must be getting something out of it – or think that you are. You are protecting yourself in some way. If we were willing to get unstuck, we'd have to let go of holding on. What exactly are we holding on to? And what would happen if we let go? Well, for starters we'd have to want truth more than being right. We'd have to acknowledge that there is a healthy part of us that has brought us to this place where we can't "do this" anymore. We can't keep going on the way we've been; we realize it no longer works. Then, we'd possibly have to let go of being a victim, being right, being hurt, being better than, or being arrogant.

Only you know what you are holding on to. This is how "the truth shall set you free."

Maybe you are stuck because you are not forgiving someone. Or because you think that you need to be forgiven. Forgiveness requires blame. Blame requires judgment. Judgment is about *right / wrong* thinking. It is about either you are right, or I am right. It is about being closed-minded to the possibilities. Possibilities are the cracks in one's thinking showing us that there may be another way to look at this.

Not forgiving means that you are choosing to have your past influence your present, which will shape your future. It is about our predetermined expectations of another that went unfulfilled. Unfulfilled expectations are in our control to acknowledge and change.

Again, this is not meant to say that your feelings of hurt and disap-pointment are not valid. They certainly are and need to be honored. But if peace and happiness trump sticking with your story and to your pain, then you have a choice. Have a little willingness to look at your expecta-tions of others.

What is your story? What unpleasant feeling or situation continually comes up in your life? Is it something connected to an important experience that gives you an excuse for why you are the way you are? Is it how you were laughed at? How you felt ashamed? The reason you overeat? Write this out:

Now, what would it take to give up your story? Who would you be without this attachment to your story? Would you be successful? Happy? Healthy?

Please note: *there may be memories and thoughts that surface during this exercise for which you should consider seeking support from a trained professional. Perhaps a grief coach or therapist may best help you through honoring your self and creating a safe environment for releasing and getting unstuck. Whatever is coming up for you is ready to be released. This is your gift to you to investigate it with proper and loving support. You are worth it!*

DEFERRED JOYS

If there were one word I would remove from the English language it is "should've." We can't "should've" anything. I recommend we replace that word with "could've." *Should've* implies that we did something wrong and usually comes with some angst, remorse or regret. It means we ought to have done something differently. And going back to an earlier discussion, we are using our current wisdom to evaluate history.

Could've implies options: I could have done such and such, although I didn't. *Could've* suggests that there are choices to every thought, word and deed. I operate out of choice ALL of the time. And not consciously making a choice is still a choice. The more aware we become of our inner voice and how we react, the more options we will see and recognize as ours. This empowers us to choose, not operate on automatic pilot. This in turns starts to give us experience(s) to change our modus operandi. Little by little, we build up an experience bank of not reacting in a situation, but rather making a conscious choice for the outcome we want. It's like predetermining how we want to look back on this situation.

I do this often with exercise. On many occasions, I do not feel like going for a run. However, I imagine what I will feel like when I am finished my run and that motivates me to tie up my laces. I also do this in conversations. Sometimes, when interacting with certain argumentative or negative individuals, my ego wants to step right in and give my two cents! I am itching to engage. I think it will feel good at that moment… and maybe it will. My shift now, however, is that I also rely on my foresight wisdom. I'm confident that tomorrow I will realize I could have made a different choice in this moment, so I make that different choice now. I've now learned through a significant experience bank that by not reacting, I will experience deferred joy.

When I was a teen, I got to hear Bishop Fulton Sheen talk at my church, Sacred Heart, in Vineland, NJ. One of the things he said stuck with me all my life: "Deferred joys, purchased by sacrifice, are the sweetest." Throughout my life, I have come to realize the truth and strength in this statement.

Sacrifice is often only thought of as loss. I prefer to think of it as giving something up in order to get something better. (Like giving up instant gratification of reacting, for internal peace tomorrow.) In all honesty, I am really only giving up something that does not serve my highest good or greatest peace and love anyway. That is my kind of sacrifice, letting go of something that I will be delighted, later, to have lost.

My father used to say don't do in haste that which you will regret in leisure. This is exactly the point. Reacting is what we do in haste. Then later (in leisure) we say we *should* have done it differently and go down the spiral, revisiting the scenario over and over again, beating ourselves up.

Can you recall a time when you've reacted in the heat of the moment and later wished you handled it differently? Can you apply one of these principles (either deferred joys or my father's saying) to that situation and see where it might have been a useful tool?

What about going forward? Can you see how this could be a loving and powerful way to support yourself?

Try This

Write out how using deferred joys could serve your highest good. Be specific in your example:

What are two things you could start to do today to support your deferred joy?

1. ....

....

....

2. ....

....

....

Was there resistance to this exercise? If so, no judgment! Just notice you have resistance. Remember, resistance is a form of fear. It is a shrewd way to keep one stuck. It is sneaky and makes you feel justified in staying stuck.

Knowing today that I have this kind of power to affect my future is exciting. Here are some examples of deferred joys:

- Think about credit card debt. I would first save up for whatever it is I wanted to purchase and not use a credit card. My sacrifice would be to control my spending piecemeal so that I could afford to buy my item without paying interest or fees on a credit card.
- Think about weight loss. Tomorrow, I will be glad I did not eat the cake or dessert today. After a series of these kinds of deferred joys, I may drop a pound or two.
- And lastly, think about holding back your opinion in a heated discussion with family. Tomorrow, will you be glad you didn't add fuel to the fire? (Even though your opinion was probably the right one...)

Deferred joys are deliberate. Deferred joys are a conscious decision. Often, our inner voice tells us that we need to react right away because we fear we only have this one quick moment to be heard. We believe this is the only chance we will have.

I learned from both of my sons that this is not the case. The eldest, Thomas, would often revisit an earlier conversation and provide additional insight. I loved this about him. The topic, from his perspective, didn't have to be over once we stopped talking about it, (whether naturally through the topic changing or if we were disagreeing). We could hit the pause button and collect our thoughts. I noticed that as long as he felt heard and respected, he was willing to revisit the topic.

My other son, Eric, was a bit more challenging. I learned to not give my opinion early (or at all) in the conversation, but rather listen, maybe ask questions and validate his story. Only later, (taking a page from Thomas' book) could I revisit the conversation with Eric.

Removing the immediacy of my needing to be heard, give my opinion, or fix something for them, I propped open the door for future discussions. I am only responsible for me. I need to be accountable to me. Understanding this allows me to operate in a way that ensures deferred joys. Especially since what I'm giving up is not serving me well anyway.

Sometimes we feel the need to provide our thoughts and feedback immediately because they bubble up, and we don't know what else to do. It is important to know and appreciate that this is how your body communicates with you. Understanding this is key. Every feeling is our body's communication system in action. Pay attention to what information is being given you. Take it in, pause and question your thoughts. Know that you "need do nothing" as *A Course In Miracles* teaches.

You are entitled to deferred joys. Learn how best to "purchase" them. And remember "don't do in haste that which you'll regret in leisure."

RUMBLE STRIPS

In the last couple of years, I've noticed that on the edge of highways and before tollbooth areas the road surface changes. It has an organized uneven pattern that is quite disruptive to the car and passengers versus the smooth surface of the highway. I call these rumble strips. My guess is that they are intentionally placed there to alert the driver to the upcoming toll or to get the driver's attention that they are driving off the road. Rumble strips provide a contrast that enhances our ability to notice.

If you've ever driven on these, you know how uncomfortable they are. And they do get your attention. I would imagine, though, if this were all you ever drove on, you would get used to it. Eventually, it would become the norm. Most likely it is not good for our ears or on the tires; however, it is what you have become used to, so you stay there.

We have these same rumble strips in life. Our bodies or our circumstances communicate with us through emotional or physical rumble strips, and it is meant to get our attention. It is our internal alert system that something needs my attention. Due to the dis-comfort or dis-ease that it creates, we may choose to ignore it.

Imagine if we did this in our car. As we are riding off the road, we ignore the rumble strips and just keep going until a crash eventually gets our attention. We don't need the crash if we pay attention to the earlier, subtler signs.

We become used to our bodies' unhealthiness or disruptive ways of being and just stay there. The crash is not the first time we can pay attention. The earlier rumbling can be our cue that a shift is needed, we are off the path of peace and happiness. Many times though we are too busy with the trivial things to really pay attention. Then we need the crash.

Most of us think we would choose to avoid a crash if we could. Yet our actions do not support our words. We ride on the rumble strip of life thinking the crash won't happen to us, or that this is just how it has always been and will never change.

What does riding the rumble strip of life look like?

- Unhappiness
- Lack of inner peace
- Short temper
- Unkindness
- Negative thinking
- Negative speaking
- Impatience
- Anger
- Dis-ease
- Arrogance
- .... (you fill in)

We can and will stay on the rumble strip of life until it no longer serves us. It sounds funny to think that we would choose to stay in something uncomfortable, and yet this happens. Choosing to ignore or stay ignorant of our body's communication system is still a choice. Choosing to blame others for our circumstances is a choice. This kind of choice is muddied by our unquestioned thoughts and lack of awareness, and it is my hope that through this book we will learn to be at ease with questioning every thought, will learn to pay attention to how our bodies feel and will start to love ourselves like we matter, because we do!

This is not ever to say that we asked for harmful events or disappointments of any kind in our life. Absolutely not. But now we can realize, with compassion, that our thoughts keep us on the rumble strip of unhappiness, blame and victimhood. None of which are how we are meant to live this life.

The contrast of rumble strips comes in all forms. For some it may be another person. Let's not kill the messenger though! Rumble strips (the messenger) themselves are not bad. It's our riding them that is unpleasant. While I prefer to never have or feel them, I now welcome the rumble strips in my life because I realize they serve a purpose; they provide a contrast that we need. They deliver a message. They get our attention and help us progress in the self-love arena. They remind us that we are off-task or not honoring our integrity in some way. Don't be angry with the teacher because you don't like the lesson.

I welcome these loving reminders that I am harming myself in some way, that I am creating dis-ease and that I have options before a crash. If I pretend I'm not on the rumble strip and resist moving off of it, I am in a constant state of bumpiness.

So what if we've already crashed? In the classroom of life, that would be called a difficult lesson, and one that you eventually master. You now are ready to deal with the consequences from the crash and move on. Dealing with the consequences in no way involves beating yourself up! Newton's third law of physics states that for every action there is an equal and opposite reaction. Meaning the greater the energy of resistance or force you use, the greater the opposing energy will be.

That really ought to stop us in our tracks. The greater I resist, the greater the magnitude of the opposing force, which in this instance I am calling consequence.

What can we do? Continue to question your thoughts, revisit the rumble strips that you ignored. You will learn. Celebrate this learning while doing what needs to be done to support yourself in healing from the crash or recovering from the consequence. Gently realize that it is because of your ignorance or unwillingness to address the rumble strip in the first place that you are in this situation. This might mean making amends. It might involve the medical or psychiatric profession. It always involves forgiveness. Forgive yourself for not paying attention.

"YEAH BUT…"

I like compliments, both giving and receiving. I noticed many years ago, however, that I am uncomfortable receiving and gifted in giving. I may have been like this most of my life, I don't know. I only noticed the difficulty in receiving compliments about 15 years ago.

The way it shows up is that I make light of the kind words being spoken. I minimize the work I've done, make it seem like it was nothing special, or transfer the focus back onto the compliment- giver. As I started to pay attention to this, I observed how others were receiving my compliments or praise. Some felt as awkward as I did, but a few just said thank you and maybe smiled, touched my hand or provided some other form of endearment. They may have felt uncomfortable, I don't know. What I do know is that they accepted the praise and in return gave me a gift. Their gift to me was the joy on their faces, their smiles or maybe simply the good feeling that something was acknowledged.

When I receive a compliment, I usually think, "Yeah, but, if you really knew…" or "Yeah, but, if you could feel the way I'm feeling, you'd think differently." The "yeah, but…"'s are our inner voice minimizing something because we did it. Certainly it can't be a big deal if I did it.

Many years ago, I started running just for fun (and food control – if I ran, I realized, I didn't have to control my food intake.) I ran in college, but that was an endurance requirement on the crew team. Anyway, years after college, I picked it up again. I'd run a few miles, and when I got used to that I thought, wouldn't it be nice to run a 5k (3.1 miles)? So I did. Then after a while I thought, five miles would be a great goal. I worked up to that, which led to a 10k (6.2 miles). When I got to that point, I thought well anyone could do that, and set my sights on 10 miles. I mean 10 miles would really be an amazing accomplishment! I successfully ran 10 and again minimized the accomplishment, setting my sights on a half marathon. A half marathon! Now that would be impressive! Well, you're getting the picture… I minimized my running accomplishments all the way up to a marathon.

Thinking that just because I do something, it must be easy or is not special is a form of "yeah, but…"

How do we stay in the un-comfortableness? How do we honor ourselves, acknowledge that a compliment, a goal achieved, or praise of some kind makes us uncomfortable and not try to get rid of the feeling of being uncomfortable but rather question the thoughts that veered us to a rumble strip?

RESISTANCE

Believe it or not, resistance is our friend. When resistance comes up, it is important to pay attention and lovingly investigate. Resistance is present when we are unwilling to uncover our preconceived notions about something. Just pay attention; just notice that this is happening. When you are ready to address it, you will. Until then, know that this is an area to be revisited. As long as resistance is present, peace is inaccessible.

So, what is behind our resistance to peace? I ask it in this manner, because it is easier to answer than, "Why don't I have peace?"

When we are not in a state of peace, and we pause a moment, most likely we will realize our resistance is because we want our way, we want someone else to be/do/speak/think differently. We want a certain outcome and are arguing with reality. There is an underlying fear.

Is it worth it? Whatever the circumstance, is it worth not having peace? Peace is always there, waiting, patiently waiting for my mind to quiet and recognize its presence! Remember that! AND, importantly, refuse to hold on to thoughts that deprive you of peace! This doesn't mean to ignore or stuff your feelings – rather embrace, dig deep, understand what is behind the resistance to get to the truth.

My roommate from college, Janie Rose recently posted on Facebook: "The truth will set you free, but it will piss you off in the process." I laughed when I read this, it is so true! Anytime I feel "off" or disturbed, I need to ask, "What is my resistance to peace in this situation?"

Embrace your resistance. Resistance simply means there is more to learn. The more learning we've done, the greater the peace and ease in which we live.

I must have had significant learning in my life because I have significant ease and simplicity in my life now. When I experience resistance, I realize there is more to learn. I don't judge the resistance as bad, and I don't blame. (Or at least I am more aware when I start to blame.) With openness and curiosity, I believe I can learn with ease – even if not simple – I can learn with love and grace and gratitude. I can learn through love and through gratitude.

When I know that all is for my highest good, I release any stickiness, oughts and shoulds. Living in the "AND" of life allows for possibilities of goodness to come from unexpected places. My resistance shows me this. My resistance just gently gets my attention to point out I have an area in my life that needs attention whenever I'm ready.

Throughout this book and in doing the exercises, has there been resistance to anything? Has there been resistance in sharing your true self with another? Or maybe the better question to ask is not if there has been resistance, rather where has there been resistance?

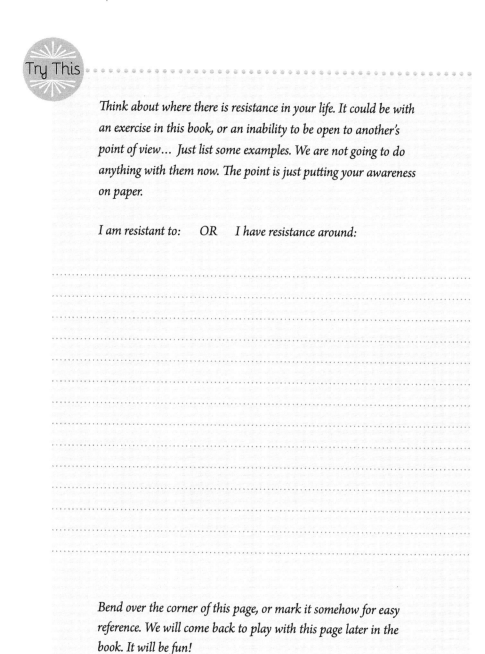

Try This

Think about where there is resistance in your life. It could be with an exercise in this book, or an inability to be open to another's point of view... Just list some examples. We are not going to do anything with them now. The point is just putting your awareness on paper.

I am resistant to: OR   I have resistance around:

Bend over the corner of this page, or mark it somehow for easy reference. We will come back to play with this page later in the book. It will be fun!

CHAPTER THREE

ALL SIDES

CONNECTED BALANCE

For the most part, what we say to ourselves about ourselves spills out and sways our thoughts and attitudes about things outside ourselves. What we think about our external world influences our inner being, our peace. Our outer world is a reflection of our inner world. We may think of these two worlds as separate, yet it is all connected. We can try, but as far as the critic/coach goes, we cannot really compartmentalize. We need to balance our inner world with our outer world. The two are together as one, and our inner dictates the outer.

In general, we may think we can either participate or observe. However, there is a third option: participate AND observe. This third option allows me to engage and intentionally not get attached to outcomes, take the higher ground, and stay aware.

Being involved in a conversation or activity is important on the human level, just as observing is important on the spiritual one. Observing requires that we look at the same situation from a higher perspective, from a bird's eye view to see the larger picture. This can play a wonderful role in how we participate, possibly shifting how we interact, creating more loving and supportive ways to engage with ourselves and then others.

When we shift our interaction, the dynamic of the situation will shift as well. When we take a higher viewpoint, we get out of our own way for the highest good of all.

Taking a higher view on matters supports our balance. When we have internal balance, it shows in our outer world. How we feel inside directly influences our outward view, demeanor and actions. I liken it to someone walking on a tightrope. Imagine the inner calm and confidence it takes to steadily walk on that rope. Imagine the deliberation of each step. Complete awareness of the foot/rope relationship, knowing that the whole body is involved. There is balance of excitement and confidence, nervousness and calm. AND, of course, this takes practice!

There must be a balance within us to walk steadily and beautifully in life as well. An inner calm that helps us to be deliberate in all our steps, words, actions, and thoughts! Imagine deliberate thoughts! Imagine paying close attention to our thoughts to ensure they bring us balance and calm and peace. This, too, takes practice! Practice is key for anything we want to master. AND our whole body is involved: what we say, what we hear (Music? Radio news?), what we watch (TV? Internet?), what we touch, how we nourish our bodies...etc...

It just takes a little willingness and practice to choose balance within by paying attention to your thoughts. Are they loving and supportive? Choose to focus: Am I creating an environment for me to flourish?

SITUATIONAL HAPPINESS

The goal (for me and those I coach) is not to have positive self-talk be dependent upon anything external. It is to learn how to treat ourselves regardless of the circumstances around us. It is to realize that we are whole and worthy just as we are. This is not to say that growth is undesirable, rather that I am lovable just as I am. In finding and acknowledging this self-love, I will want to be a self-coach, not a critic. I may not be *perfect*, but who defines what that is anyway? And why would I allow my past, pop culture, tabloids, fashion magazines or my critic voice to define anything?

Knowing I am worthy just as I am becomes like an upward spiral attracting more awareness, opening up new channels for coaching thoughts, and quieting our critic voice.

Over the years in business consulting and coaching, I've had many clients. Two in particular come to mind, both suffering from what I call "situational happiness." They appeared to have a Jekyll/Hyde personality, truly erratic behavior. The hardest thing to know is who would show up for a meeting or be on a conference call. From what was shared with me, they were mostly disliked by colleagues and often feared by subordinates. They were unpleasant to be around if things weren't going their way. This is hardly the way to behave to get the most out of employees; however, that's a topic for another book.

I had a gentle compassion toward them and would often think how hard it must be to be them. It seemed to me it couldn't be easy to be at the mercy of external things to determine your level of peace and happiness.

Can you relate to this? Can you think of things outside of yourself that are the source of your happiness? Complete this statement:

I know I would be happy if:

1. . . . .

2. . . . .

3. . . . .

4. . . . .

Look back on the list. Are these things you can buy with money? Is it money itself? Are these things you can cover with insurance? Are these things outside of you in any way?

If you answered yes, then you have situational happiness. Your happiness is dependent upon things out of your control and external to you. These are fleeting and are subject to change.

This exercise was done to support you on your journey, not make you feel bad about yourself. Once we have awareness, we bring things from our subconscious to our consciousness. We can then shed light and grow in our understanding and awareness.

SACREDNESS

My father and I used to talk about the subtleties of seeing. He would often say that I had a gift to see things *glass half-full* and that this would serve me well in life. He and I were very alike in this way. In a letter he wrote to me more than 10 years ago, he talked about "Everyday Sacredness." In that letter, he said, "I truly believe you personify this type of spirituality. You constantly have an awareness about the very sacred dimension of everyday life."

While I am humbled by his comment (and it took some time for my inner voice to not dismiss his lovely and powerful observation), I can't help but think there **is** a sacred dimension to everything and everyone. We just need to be open to awareness and look for evidence of this sacredness.

Imagine if every day we became aware of the choice we have to see all through the lens of this sacred dimension – and then became willing to do so? What if we saw all as sacred? If I saw my thoughts and actions as sacred, wouldn't I have to pay attention to my thoughts? Wouldn't I pursue investigation as suggested earlier in Chapter Two? Not in a judgmental way, but with curiosity, openness and gentleness.

We consider something sacred if we hold it in great respect and reverence. If we held ourselves in great respect, we wouldn't tolerate toxicity in our life. If we revered ourselves, not in an egoistic way, rather with a depth of holiness, it would be simpler to do so for others. The greater love we have for ourselves, the greater we can have for others. Loving ourselves is not about materialism, it is not showy or flashy, rather it is demonstrated only by our thoughts and actions about and toward ourselves.

When our love cup is full, the overflow can go to others, and will be seen by others in our attitude and energy. When our love cup is less than full, we need to fill it. *I am the only one who can fill my love cup.* This looks like positive self-talk, meditation, investigation and being my best friend.

It is impossible for another to fill your love cup. That kind of filling is temporary, superficial, and leaves you seeking outside of yourself to fill up. (I think therapists call this type of unhealthy relationship co-dependency.) It is what addictions are made from, seeking externally to change an internal feeling. Oh, this *seems* to work – that's why we do it. We spend money to feel better, take a drink to feel better, zone out in front of the TV to just be able to feel somehow differently than we do. It is instant gratification. It is called that because it is gratifying only for that instant, then we need more. That which we seek in order to feel better actually worsens the situation, leaving us empty and in need of more filling. It is a vicious cycle that causes us to want more of that which was not satisfying to begin with.

It is impossible for another to fill your love cup. That kind of filling is temporary, superficial, and leaves you seeking outside of yourself to fill up. (I think therapists call this type of unhealthy relationship co-dependency.) It is what addictions are made from, seeking externally to change an internal feeling. Oh, this *seems* to work – that's why we do it. We spend money to feel better, take a drink to feel better, zone out in front of the TV to just be able to feel somehow differently than we do. It is instant gratification. It is called that because it is gratifying only for that instant, then we need more. That which we seek in order to feel better actually worsens the situation, leaving us empty and in need of more filling. It is a vicious cycle that causes us to want more of that which was not satisfying to begin with.

My aunt, a Maryknoll nun, who was taken prisoner of war in WWII, used to say that this generation is filled with "exaggerated busy-ness." We would discuss how in this 21st century, people look outside of themselves to get and to feel happiness, how they avoid being unplugged and avoid being in silence with just themselves. Her thought was that if they spent time with themselves, they wouldn't like what they found. She lived to be 104. She liked herself. She knew how to fill her self-love cup so that she could spend over a century caring for and loving others.

I like myself. I unplug. I no longer seek externally. (Well, at least most of the time, and I catch myself quicker now.) I could be stuck at an airport with no devices, just me, and I would enjoy it. My friend from college whom we called "Y'all" used to say I could be my own best company. I like that!

Do you like yourself? Do you respect yourself?

Try This

Sit quietly, relax and take in three deep breaths through your nose. Close your eyes and hold yourself in a loving space. Let yourself know you want to come from a place of compassion and kindness. Find out if you like yourself – stay in the stillness. Pay attention to what comes up. Tears are okay! Smiles are okay! Both are great!

If you experienced a moment of sadness or a feeling that is just not a happy one, be kind to yourself! This is the time for hidden emotions and thoughts to surface. This is not about judging; rather, it is meant to be revealing and healing. Ask yourself how you can come to like yourself. What words are suggested for you to say (or stop saying) to yourself to help with this process.

- *In what ways do you sabotage your love for yourself?*
- *In what ways can you show yourself love?*
- *In what ways are you sacred?*

Write these out:

Then write out something you will start to do every day that is loving to you. What action or thought or prayer will you demonstrate
a willingness to do?

When done, thank yourself for caring about you.
Tell yourself: I Love You.

If you experienced elation, thank yourself. Ask what else you can do to stay in love with yourself – to keep your friendship going? Write these out:

....

....

....

....

....

....

....

....

....

Then write out something new you can start to do every day that is loving to you. What action or thought or prayer will you demonstrate a willingness to do for you?

....

....

....

....

....

....

....

....

....

....

When done, thank yourself for caring about you.
Tell yourself: I Love You.

MAKING SNOWFLAKES

When things are going well, we feel energized, seem to have a good outlook on life and have a general sense of happiness. Often the opposite is true as well. When things are not going our way, we often feel drained, bummed-out and maybe even a bit depressed.

What makes something "go our way" or not? It is our pre-determined, inflexible thoughts about the situation. We often don't even realize that we have set up an expectation or outcome and yet when it is unfulfilled (and unexamined), we feel it... in our body, possibly, and in our energy level. Our mood shifts, and the voice in our head goes wild with chatter and commentary about the situation.

There is no judgment here, just a call out for awareness. What is important to recognize is that our thoughts dictate our mood, our body physically responds to our thoughts. Our thoughts are what matter most. If we can modify and impact our thoughts, the rest will follow.

When we are inflexible and think there is only one right outcome in a situation, we will struggle when that outcome does not happen. We have left no room for possibility. Our mind chatter will take over and we will physically respond to the thoughts and words being used to mentally evaluate the situation, our role in it and the others involved.

Dr. Emoto[1], a Japanese scientist, devoted his life to studying the impacts of our thoughts. One way he accomplished this was to expose water to words like *Peace, I Love You, Love and Gratitude, I Hate You, I'll Kill You, Mother Teresa, Hitler.* He even exposed water to songs like "Imagine" by John Lennon and hard rock. After freezing the water, he examined the water molecules and found that water exposed to the negatively charged words was deformed, dark and blob-like; it was unpleasant to the eye. The water exposed to the positively charged words was symmetrical and snowflake-like, full of airiness and light; it was beautiful to see.

This is astounding research. Could this be why we physically feel better when we are with positive people and situations? Since we are made up of somewhere between 50-80 percent water, it makes sense that we would have a physical response to negative/positive influences as well as the critic/coach voice. Are we making internal snowflakes? Are we creating these symmetrical beauties in our bodies with our own thoughts or are we creating dark, ugly blobs?

What words do we expose ourselves to every day beyond our inner critic? Through TV, the Internet, radio, music, co-workers, friends, family, what words do we allow our mind and body to be exposed to? We know this kind of exposure is not good for children, so we have parental controls. We wouldn't want a young child to be exposed to hard-core porn or violent scenes in a movie or harsh cursing in a song. We would protect our children from listening or seeing offensive things, yet we voluntarily allow ourselves this negative or toxic exposure. We may not have a choice regarding what is on TV; however, we have a choice to watch or not.

I recently read on Politifact.com that over 50% of Fox News is mostly false or false. I didn't verify the quantitative data, but what I have observed over the years when watching a clip (not intentionally) is that those on that station seem to be very angry, unhappy people. They ooze unpleasantness, seem very argumentative and are definitely people with whom I would never choose to be stuck at an airport.

There is no judgment, no critic voice in this. Just an awareness that my snowflakes shift to dark blobs when I have this kind of exposure. This is what we are meant to realize for ourselves. Are we getting riled up and angry, or are we growing in compassion? Are we making or destroying our snow-flakes? Do we pay attention to our body's response and our inner voice to know what is healthy for us?

Once our inner voice becomes the coach, we will lovingly know how to make snowflakes and remove ourselves from toxic situations and angry people, whether Fox News, a negative relationship or the critic in our mind. The key is strengthening the coach voice and unleashing it, all the while gently silencing the critic voice.

Make snowflakes.

FOLLOW THE LEADER

Several years ago, I took six-week break from my blog to write some magazine articles for the Mind, Body and Soul section of *American Nurse Today*. What I realized during that time though is that I never took a break from my run-on brain-babble thoughts. This constant stream of words, discernment, judgment, evaluation, thoughts, ideas, opinions, brainstorms just kept going on and on and on, blah, blah, blah. I wondered how to get a break. This is the purpose of meditation, to get into a place of non-thought.

The important thing is my awareness that this happens. In the moment of *brain babble*, I can choose to acknowledge the words being mentally formed, the thoughts that follow and allow them to pass. To do this, I must be in a conscious and constant state of AWARENESS that it is happening! Awareness is the key to shifting any pattern of behavior, so when a thought appears, I can choose to not follow it or attach to it.

I can choose! When aware, I have the choice to *follow* the thought or **lead** the thought. When I follow, I am reactive. To lead a thought, I must change positions with it, gently question it, and with compassion, determine its truthfulness and purposefulness. I do this by asking myself:

~ It this thought true? Am I being honest or judgmental?

~ Does it serve my highest good?

~ How is this thought useful to another or me?

Often this type of inquiry is annoying in the midst of a heated discussion, but I know through my foresight wisdom, I will appreciate this later. It's like having hindsight vision now.

When I do this simple inquiry, I am able to reach a higher ground perspective. Only from this higher place am I able to lead my thoughts or at least quiet them.

I like to play "Follow the Leader" with my thoughts, and I want to be the leader. I want to lead my thoughts! AND as soon as I realize I've started following again, I will express gratitude for the awareness, do a little dance in celebration of my awareness and move to the leader spot again!

And you? Interested in playing the game today? Willing to be the leader? You know yourself and your thoughts better than anyone. What questions are best suited for you to ask yourself to determine the truthfulness and purposefulness of your thoughts?

Try This

Think of two or three questions you could ask yourself when you are feeling the rumble strips of life and realize your thoughts are in the lead. Start with mine if you want and make changes as best suit you. Write these out:

Use these today. Put these questions on a piece of paper and put it in your pocket to have throughout the day. Put them on your dashboard. Put them on your bathroom mirror. Memorize them and use them often.

MASKS AND CAGES

Oh, the things we do to maintain and protect our persona and hide who we really are! What is it that we fear so much in showing our true beautiful God-like selves? Are we so cemented in righteousness, prejudice or going-along-to-get-along that we forget our roots of divinity?

At Halloween, we dress up and wear costumes intended to hide who we are from others. We get to play a role. Masks certainly help in this fun endeavor. Some costumes are wonderful at hiding our whole head and body, while some only cover parts of our face. Our masks may simply be creative makeup worn to disguise us.

There is another kind of mask we can wear. Sometimes we wear masks in our professional or everyday lives. We have certain roles we play that may not be who we really are. Certain qualities we possess may not be "welcomed" or thought of as "appropriate" like compassion – or empathy – or honesty. So we have to hide ourselves to fit in or be thought of in a certain way.

I am so grateful that most of the time I no longer wear a mask. I am living in authenticity. I live in alignment with my standards of integrity as best I can, no pretense allowed, no pretending required. When I come from a place of authenticity, I practice the art of allowing. I allow you to be you and me to be me. I accept that we all are doing the best we can at any moment. I don't need anything external to change for me to feel in alignment.

This does not mean that I will allow others to mistreat me, or that I pursue a deeper relationship with everyone I meet, especially if our energy fields seem to be mismatched. This does mean, however, that I remove judgment. I honor my "god-guide" that some investigation may be needed on my part, and I have loving thoughts for each of us on our journeys.

There is a difference between being aware of what serves my highest good and being stuck – whether through co-dependency or trying to *fix* someone! We all are on our individual journeys! I do not know your path. I trust that we all are exactly where we need to be, even if that means someone wearing a mask. The mask is worn until it is not! It is not my responsibility to remove your mask; however, if you want to do this, I certainly will support your process.

What is important to note is not the mask, but rather the awareness of the mask. The mask worn on others or us may come with judgment. The awareness comes with choice.

In addition to wearing our masks in an attempt to hide our true selves, we all live in a cage made up of our limiting thoughts. For some it is very narrow; for others it may be roomier. The walls of our cages are made up of our beliefs, our thoughts and our judgments. It is how we interpret our world.

When we bump up against the edges of our cage, we experience discomfort of some kind. The greater our steadfastness to "right and wrong" thinking and "my way is the only way," the greater our discomfort and angst, and the more we suffer. The choice is to feel the discomfort, question our thoughts and possibly break down that barrier – OR to move away from the edge, back into our cage, solidify the barrier and cage ourselves in even more.

The question becomes, are you willing to expand your cage? Are you willing to weaken the walls for greater freedom from thought or perhaps just widen it a bit to make it roomier?

Notice today when you feel discomfort about something someone says or does, or the way they are dressed, and challenge your thoughts. Break down a barrier to break through. Expand your cage.

THE MOST IMPORTANT HUMAN RELATIONSHIP

I cannot do for others that which I cannot do for myself! I cannot participate in an outer relationship to a greater degree than I participate in my inner relationship. We may think we can, however we are greatly limited. And, possibly, we are resentful and angry if we are asked to give more outside of ourselves than TO ourselves. (Which has NOTHING to do with the other person... it has to do with us not being fully engaged in the most important relationship first!)

What are the ways to create a deeper relationship with me? It is no different than what we would do with ANY relationship we want to cultivate. We call, we *support*, we *listen*, we **love**, we invite, we **nurture**, we *spend time with*, we say "I'm sorry"... get it? These are ALL the things to do with and for us!

How are the ways I support and love myself? Do I clothe my body warmly on chilly days? Do I nurture the organs of my body well – or think junk food will support it? Do I talk to myself supportively – or am I a constant critic? Do I listen to negativity or violence on TV and expose myself to this kind of lower energy? Do I listen to what my body is telling me? Do I spend quiet time in meditation?

There are many ways to rekindle the relationship with ourselves. The *Try This* exercises in this book are intended to rekindle your relationship with you. When we've done all the exercises and gone back and reflected on them again, maybe we can start with an "I'm sorry I haven't been there for you lately..." and take us out for a long walk and talk!

The thing is, your inner you is with you all the time. This is your spirit. Ignoring it doesn't make it go away... it only makes you feel and react in ways not loving and peaceful. Someone once told me the only things that go away when ignored are your teeth.

Ignoring things keeps us ignorant. Investigating removes the veil of ignorance. It helps us to break through our resistance to change, our resistance to growth and wanting things our way. Remember the *Try This* exercise you did on resistance? Let's play with that some more, since now you know it will deepen the most important human relationship, your relationship with you.

It is said that what we resist will persist. This is because we put energy into the resistance. Anything we put energy into stays alive. We keep it alive through our resistance. It's like the game of tug-of-war; the game can only stay alive if both sides are holding onto the rope. We are holding onto a rope, resisting the other side, pulling it, wanting to win, and in the process we put a lot of energy into that. But if I let go, the resistance is no longer there; it no longer holds me. My relationship with me is not a game of tug-of-war. Am I willing to open my hand and release the ropes that bind and tether me?

Try This

Sit quietly, relax and take in three deep breaths through your nose. Close your eyes and hold yourself in a loving space. Let yourself know you want to come from a place of compassion and kindness.

Go back and look at your list of resistances from the exercise in the Resistance section of this book. Gently ask yourself why you have resistance on each one. You don't have to give up your resistance; I'm just asking that you pay attention and be honest with yourself. Often times the first answer is "just because," which really just means you want your own way, and you're stubborn. Or you may find that you have a prejudice about the situation. Just be honest.

Now ask yourself how you would feel if this resistance was gone?
How would you feel if you had peace about this?

I want you to bookmark this page. Go ahead – fold down the top corner or somehow mark this page. Once you have finished the book, come back and revisit this list. You may have greater insight into your resistance. Just because the book is finished doesn't mean your learning is done.

For today, be vigilant about what you say and do. Pay attention to areas of resistance. Just acknowledge that they are there. Think about the imaginary rope in your hand. Have a good time with you, whatever the circumstance. As the L'Oreal commercial says – "I'm worth it." I am. You are too. You are so very worth it. Be your own L'Oreal commercial. And when you are ready, you'll open your hand, confident that release far outweighs resistance.

AHA MOMENTS

We all know what these are. These are moments when the light bulb switches on. For some reason, we instantly have a greater awareness. We can see something or realize something that just moments before we were blind to.

Think of AHA as being an acronym for **A H**eightened **A**wareness.

AHA moments are the universe's gift to us. It is like the veil of ignorance was peeled back just long enough for us to see differently. Once we have this kind of moment, we are forever changed. We cannot go back to our previous ignorance.

Sometimes this happens when we are given additional information about a situation. Prior to the additional information, we had *thoughts* and opinions. Then with added information we can see a bigger picture.

So, how can we create and master AHA? Well, we can't know what we don't know; however, we can be open to the possibility that we don't know all there is to know. This may sound simple, but if it were, we'd all be doing it. This would require us to live in constant curiosity that there is more than what we think. We would need to evaluate all that we hold as true. And, importantly, see from a bird's eye view.

This would almost look like a triangle with the base being our current linear way of thinking, and the opposite ends of the base being differing or opposing views. As these connect up to the tip of the triangle, I am able to see a greater picture.

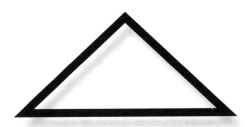

From the top, I am able to see left and right, good and bad, right and wrong, all of it. What we pay attention to is what we will see. From the top of the triangle, it looks like the rays of a flashlight or headlight shining out. Using a flashlight while on just the base of the triangle, I only see where I'm pointing. Shining it down from the top sheds light on a much greater area, helping me to see more.

In seeing a greater portion of the story, I am acutely aware that without this vision, I am limited. Every time we come from a place of limited vision, our understanding is inaccurate at best.

AHAs are created from the top tip. There is a fine line between judgment and discernment. Judgment lacks AHAs; it lacks inquiry and requires "right versus wrong" thinking. Discernment is all about AHAs because it is about investigation and questioning so that I can learn more.

The goal is to start to step away from judgment and into a place of investigation, a place of questioning, a place that allows room for me to dig deeper without flogging myself in the process. In this investigation, I grow. I learn and am pushed through the sometimes-cramped darkness of the birth canal into a place of openness, light and clarity.

RIGHT VS. ???

When we think about things in terms of right and wrong, it is polarizing. Think back to the triangle with right and wrong being on either end of the base. If I am right then you must be wrong and vice versa. For the most part, it is preferred to be on the right side, unpleasant to be on the wrong side. No one likes to be proven wrong.

One of the clients I mentioned who experienced situational happiness was also someone who needed to be right in any situation. Although frequently wrong, she was never in doubt. This made for very tense relationships and a consistent lack of trust.

Many who study *A Course In Miracles* are often heard saying or asking, "Would you rather be right or happy?" as a way to deal with a right/wrong mentality. I have always struggled with that choice because, sometimes, being right would make me happy. I understand the thinking behind viewing it differently; however, right vs. happy doesn't work for me. Notice how I am not making anyone else wrong in this; I'm simply stating it doesn't work for me. I'm allowing it to be perfectly okay for you.

This brings me to the thought process I find most useful. It is the way in which I look at an alternative to "right /wrong" and "right / happy" thinking. I can't take credit for this though. A previous boss and mentor, Elizabeth Houlihan, shared this with me. When I would express frustration with her regarding a work-related process, she would often say "would you rather be right or *effective*?" I would choose effective every time. Her wise, non-judgmental words deeply influenced me. My goal in every situation is to be effective, not alienating, not polarizing, not drawing a line in the sand.

It is easier to be effective from the top point on the triangle. Seeing the greater perspective helps in being effective.

Effective implies successful. Your ego is put aside for a greater good. It implies that we both will feel heard, both will have our dignity remain intact. It allows space for cooperation, discussion, disagreement and respect.

When you walk away from a conversation in which "effective" was your goal, there is no residual stickiness. There is no revisiting the discussion and beating yourself up. Importantly, "effective" is filled with deferred joys.

UNPLUG, a.k.a. THE SABBATH

Every religion I can think of has recommended or required time to rest. It is interesting to note that this rest time was thought to be necessary tens of thousands of years ago. Before TVs, radios, computers, cell phones, etc... before any technology, the pure essence of human beings knew we needed to unplug and spend time with God. (I often wonder from what exactly were they unplugging? That's another topic for later.)

I'm not requiring that you believe in God, or even use that name for her. I am suggesting, however, that there is something greater than us. We are connected to it. I call this God. Our connection remains whether we think it does or not. Just like we all have lungs and breathe. We can be conscious and grateful to this life force in and for our bodies or not – it doesn't affect or matter to our lungs. We breathe anyway. Our lungs and our breath are not dependent on our belief in them.

If we are conscious, however, we have the potential to have an enhanced relationship with our lungs, our breathing and our body.

In the *Try This* exercises, I begin with three deep breaths in and out through the nose. Why? According to Dr. Christiane Northrup[2], when breathing deeply like this through your nose, your lower lungs get filled and that activates the vagus nerve. Our deep nose breaths through the vagus nerve help in digestion and restoration of our emotional body.

Only when we tame our thoughts and silence our critic voice can we truly hear what is loving and digest what is nourishing.

We are familiar with physical digestion. It is the process of breaking down that which feeds our body (food) into substances that can be used. What cannot be used is excreted.

Spiritual digestion is no different. It is the process of breaking down that which nourishes our soul. Spiritual food is love, truth, prayer, meditation, acts of kindness, inspired readings, inspired lectures, human connection, etc. This is digested into substances that can be used, which help in our awareness and light our path. That which does not serve us well (toxic things, negative people, the relationships and struggles that do not align with our standards of integrity) must be excreted and left behind.

One way to do this is to have a personal Sabbath. Whether secular or spiritual, just unplug. Take one day a week to unplug from the things of this material world and plug into something greater than you. When this day arrives, ask: how will you nourish your soul today? What will you spiritually digest today? What will strengthen and enrich your connection with God? Start with a couple of hours if the whole day seems too scary. (And, of course, that is an opportunity to have a wee chat with yourself about that thought that it might be too scary to go the whole day unplugged. Maybe go back to the very first *Try This* exercise and use this thought as the example.)

Another way is to meditate each day, start with five – 10 minutes and work your way up to 20 – 30. If we are honest with ourselves, we know can find this time. The question becomes: is it important enough?

A third way is to journal with God. Write out your thoughts and feelings, and in a Neale Donald Walsch[3] kind of way, ask questions and listen for the loving non-judgmental answers that arise.

We have no awkwardness or issues with nourishing our bodies. What about our souls? What about supporting that soft, loving voice in you that wants healing and joy and peace and love?

Our electronic toys don't last forever. Whether daily or yearly, the batteries wear low and need recharging. Some of our electronics, like TVs or lamps, don't even work if not plugged into an energy source all the time. So, too, we need to have our spiritual batteries recharged. We cannot continue to operate at peak performance, in peace and happiness, without a recharge.

We don't expect more from our electronics than they can give. If we have an unreasonable expectation, we may be left with a dead cell phone, or stranded on a highway without gas in our car. We often get warning signs before this happens. A light goes on, or an alarm goes off. Our bodies also give warning signs that we need to physically, mentally, spiritually, emotionally recharge. The warning signs are impatience, quick tempers, unhappiness, having reactions not responses, feeling overwhelmed.

Unplug. Take a personal Sabbath. Connect with God who is the greatest and most powerful recharger of all.

Try This

Sit quietly, relax and take in three deep breaths through your nose. Close your eyes and hold yourself in a loving space. Let yourself know you want to come from a place of compassion and kindness.

Think about a time when you felt spiritually and emotionally nourished. Bathe in that glorious feeling for a moment. Then think about when the opposite was true. Compare the two feelings.

Ask yourself what you think it would take for you to devote 10 minutes a day and a couple of hours on your Sabbath to recharging your batteries.

Write out how you feel when recharged and using your coach voice. Tell yourself how this could work in the upcoming week.

CHAPTER FOUR

❧

NOW WHAT?

WHAT ABOUT THEM?

Often, as we begin this deep spiritual work of nourishing and connecting to our inner coach, we notice more how others would benefit from this work too. When this happens, it is an opportunity to check in to see from where this thought arises. Is it coming from a place of knowing what we think they ought to do? Are we judging that they are not doing it right? Or does it come from a place of willingness to share your journey?

When awareness comes without judgment toward another, you will find you are more open to sharing your path and can easily release expectations that they will do what you think is best for them. When we share ourselves with a sincere and non-judgmental heart, we also create a safe place for the other. We lay the groundwork to be effective and receptive.

How others behave, how they interact, their mannerisms, words, and actions are not about you. None of it is about you. It is all about them; what is going on with their mind and soul, ego and spirit, critic and coach. How others behave simply represents being on or off the rumble strip, and coming from a place of fear or love. When we realize this, it helps to calm our inner critic and puts so many things in perspective.

What is important to notice is our thoughts about them. This is where our critic voice can get sneaky again. The greater and deeper our work, the less tolerance we have for negativity and chaos in our lives. Notice this without judgment, without right/wrong thinking. Allow room for being "effective" as discussed at the end of Chapter Three.

STILLNESS

In a world filled with instant gratification, instant communication and (unfortunately) instant pudding, one needs to make time for stillness. How ironic is that? We must plan to be still. Plan to have downtime. Why? Because diversions are profound in this 21st century, and we mostly play in the tiny sandbox called distraction.

Stillness is what will nourish our soul, strengthen our inner coaching voice and rejuvenate our core. Stillness is what clears our minds and allows healing and forgiveness to seep into the nooks and crannies of our hearts.

To hear our coaching voice we first need to be still. It is the conscious act of letting go of the turbulence (or critic) in our minds. I find through meditation and prayer I can easily get to a place of tranquility, and this practice builds that ability. This is what nurtures my inner coach.

Just as my body needs nourishment to sustain itself, so too does my soul. I think there is a direct link between my inner coach and my soul. I can only imagine how God tries to get our attention so that we can see ourselves the way He does. As a parent, I want my children to see themselves through my eyes: filled with potential, love and greatness. I want this to sustain them until they get to a place of being able to nourish and coach themselves enough so that their internal eyesight and voice is loving. I imagine that this is what God wants for us as well. But it is up to us. We get to choose how we want to show up for ourselves!

We get to make the decision to live in peace with the world around us and ourselves - or not. All it takes is a little stillness. It is so simple, yet often so difficult. Have you done any unplugging since the last section of Chapter Three?

Often we claim to want to have inner peace and the type of happiness that is not dependent on external things, yet we allow other activities or demands to get in our way. We easily get sidetracked and then wonder why we aren't successful at it. (And by now, I hope you are just observing and not criticizing yourself.) We think we are sincere in our efforts, yet seem to sabotage our very desires through activities that may be energy drains or time-wasters.

Can you help set yourself up for success? Let me give you an example. I like to run early in the morning. This is important to me. However, I know myself well enough to know that when the alarm goes off at five a.m., many mornings I will hit the snooze button until it is too late to get in the run. (This is a perfect example of my father's saying "Don't do in haste that which you'll regret in leisure" from Deferred Joys in Chapter Two.) The tool I use to set myself up for success at five a.m. during the week is named Kathy. Kathy and I have been meeting in the wee hours of the morning for 15+ years. I know if I plan to meet her for a morning run, I will get out of bed. I have set myself up for some accountability. I do the same thing on the weekends for long runs and half marathon training, meeting Pat and Judy. Who is your Kathy? Who are your Pat and Judy?

Sit quietly, relax and take in three deep breaths through your nose. Close your eyes and hold yourself in a loving space. Let yourself know you want to come from a place of compassion. Take a few moments to completely relax.

Put your phone on "block all calls" and set a timer for 10 minutes. Just sit with your eyes closed for 10 minutes. If thoughts come in, just let them pass by. If you need to, count your slow breaths up to four and repeat over and over.

When the timer goes off, you are done.

How did this feel? Was it hard to just be quiet? Did your mind want to continually engage in something? Was having the timer on to let you know when the 10 minutes were up helpful?

Are you willing to this exercise again tomorrow for 15 minutes? Why or why not? If there is resistance, do you know why? Are you uncomfortable with just yourself? If you are willing to this again tomorrow, was there a sense of accomplishment and delight today?

···
···
···
···
···
···
···
···
···
···
···

Are you willing to have a partner to help with accountability?
Who would that be? Can you use foresight wisdom and imagine
the feeling of success? What does it feel like?

···
···
···
···
···
···
···
···
···
···
···
···
···
···

Never underestimate the power of shutting up and shutting off. These two simple acts give way to the possibility of contemplation. Contemplation is attentive consideration of our circumstances, our lifestyle, our thoughts, our way of being and ultimately our actions. So, let me repeat: in the stillness of contemplation, we get to choose how we want to show up for ourselves, every time!

EPILOGUE

What I've come to realize and appreciate is that everyone does their best with what they know and believe to be true at any given time. I know I am doing the best I can, so why wouldn't I extend that same thought process to you? Why would I hold you to a different set of expectations than I do for myself? Because the thoughts in my head told me so. My made-up version of how others ought to behave differs from reality, and instead of questioning my thoughts, I make you wrong.

If we look at others as doing their best for what they know today, it offers us kindness toward them and the situation. It allows space for all of us to be at different places on our path. «Different» does not mean right or wrong, good or bad; it is just *not the same* as me!

When I make you wrong, then you are to blame for my uncomfortable feelings. As soon as I place blame, the downward spiral begins. However (and this is important!), if we can catch ourselves at the moment our reality does not meet our expectations and investigate our expectations, our eyes begin to open. Eye-opening experiences lead to AHA moments, which, when coupled with compassion and kindness toward the situation and ourselves, leads to greater awareness, growth, and inner peace.

Often people think that if they are living in this awareness and are growing from this spiritual perspective that they ought to have perfect, loving relationships 100 percent of the time. I think we can practice loving responses all the time, but we need to also release expectations and question our thoughts about the person or situation. I believe others come into our lives for a reason or a season. It is our unquestioned thoughts that are the cause of our expecting something different. Still, sometimes it is hard to let go.

We have these invisible hollow cords that connect each of us to others and help form our relationships. When a relationship is complete (perhaps you use the word "over"), be it through choice or not (ie: death, break-up), sometimes the invisible cords of connection remain.

Before I talk more about the invisible cord, I want to mention my use of the word "complete" versus "over" in my statement "when a relationship is complete…" Whenever we complete something, we acknowledge a finality, sometimes with a sense of accomplishment, and move to the next door opening. For example, we complete grade school and move on to high school. We complete an exam and become certified in a field. We complete holiday shopping and celebrate the holidays with gift giving. The word "complete" acknowledges thoroughness in reaching a potential while at the same time removing judgment.

So, back to the cords. When a relationship is complete, sometimes the invisible cords of connection remain. The invisible cords of connection can be a drain if the cords are ones of fear, anger, hurt, resentment or "should've" – and these cords need to be cut – with kindness, by being willing to investigate our thoughts and wanting peace. These cords are energy drains. The umbilical cord, when its function is COMPLETE, must be cut for the greatest good, indeed the survival, of mother and child. So too in relationships that are complete. For the greatest good of all involved, the cord that no longer serves a loving peaceful purpose must be cut.

Only cords of love, compassion, peace and joy can sustain. These cords may remain – loving, tender, compassionate energy flows through these.

Sit quietly, relax and take in three deep breaths through your nose. Close your eyes and hold yourself in a loving space. Let yourself know you want to come from a place of compassion, kindness and honesty. Take a look at some of the relationships in your life that are complete, yet the invisible cord are still intact, cords that might be energy drains, cords that are not sustaining, but rather holding you back. Choose just one relationship. Think about the purpose this relationship had in your life. What growth opportunities were given you? What inner strength came about?

Say to yourself, "Joyfully, I shall release the connection to my relationship with .... by cutting the cord, with compassion and love, for them and for me. I honor that until __this__ very moment, it served a purpose, and I am very grateful for recognizing its purpose in my life." Visualize cutting the cord saying, "As it is complete, I am complete."

What was the purpose of holding on to that relationship?

....

....

....

....

....

....

....

....

Can you see that it is complete?
How does it feel to allow it to be complete?

Seasons change. Is there anything we can do about it? No! Seasons change; that is what they do. Some climate zones change severely and some mildly, some with hardly a visible change at all. It is what they do, without my help, worry, reporting, enjoying, playing or anything else. Our choice is to witness, to allow, to enjoy and marvel... (or not)

Our thoughts are like the seasons. We have them. Thoughts appear; that's what they do. Not much we can do about them, except be a witness to them (top of triangle), investigate, acknowledge they are there and let them be, without having to engage in or react to them.

Some thoughts are harsh and severe, some are mild, some loving. Some thoughts are the same tape playing over and over and over again, so much so that we don't even recognize they are there. They control our mood, self-worth and our interactions. And without awareness, we stay believing in them, with all their unpleasant consequences.

Thoughts do what they do... appear. We, however, can choose to activate them and engage through inquiry, or we can just notice the thought and chuckle at its coming to play with us. We can choose to play with the thought or not. Every time! Engage with the thoughts that love and produce a smile. Leave the sandbox of thoughts that are fear and worry based. Play in a different sandbox! And enjoy the season as it changes!

Bless this journey we are on. Go back and revisit the exercises in this book. Each time you do, you will uncover more love, peace and joy. Be your own L'Oreal commercial... You ARE worth it!

I love the saying: "Be kind to yourself, and your mind will become kind as well. That's how it works." ~ Adyashanti. It is how it works. It's all an inside job. The truth of the matter is that you are responsible for what you think.

Question your thoughts, re-do the exercises, choose the coach voice with kindness and compassion. Our minds are very powerful and we are much too tolerant of mind-wandering, blaming and criticizing. Being aware of our thoughts is very old wisdom.

First century, BCE philosopher, Lao-Tze said:

Watch your thoughts;
they become words.
Watch your words;
they become actions.
Watch your actions;
they become habits.
Watch your habits;
they become character.

Understanding this is foundational to any spiritual or personal growth. It shapes who we are and the legacy we will leave to our children and beyond. Dream big, love large, quiet the critic and care for the coach.

One last exercise! Although slightly modified, this exercise was originally created by my friend Lizzie Rose and written here with permission.

Write out three of your dreams, three things you'd like to achieve, or that maybe have been secret aspirations. No self-imposed boundaries, just quickly list these:

1. ....

2. ....

3. ....

Great! Isn't it fun to think about our dreams and aspirations?

Choose one specific dream of yours from the three that you listed and circle it. Put stars around it too! Now write out three things you tell yourself about why you cannot achieve this aspiration or goal. These are three things that your critic voice uses to remind you why this dream will not be realized.

It is what keeps you stuck.

1. ....

2. ....

3. ....

Next, turn those three things around. Use your coach voice to respond to the three obstacles that your critic voice gave you. Use strong words like "I can... " or "I will... " Be your own coach!

1. ....

2. ....

3. ....

How did that feel? Do you feel a little more empowered coming from the coach point of view? Did you feel a shift in energy moving from the critic's list to the coach's list? The coach voice is not telling you things that are not true about yourself, but rather supporting you on your quest to reach your dreams! Write out how that experience felt:

Now, go out and make your dream come true.
It's only that critic voice holding you back!
Make some awesome snowflakes!

IN GRATITUDE

In no special order, it is with gratitude I acknowledge those whose love and support helped along the way. First, I want to thank the voice inside my head for all of its coaching and cheerleading. This voice has been with me all my life and I really have fun with her.

I have a loving, passionate, wild and fiercely protective family. My siblings, Jerry, Coffee-Maureen, Roland, Barbara, Barry, Stephen and Tea-Maureen, have provided a lifetime of coaching, criticizing and cheerleading… all done with the best of intentions, and I love each of you. I was blessed to have the parents I did. Love you mom and dad - and I miss my dad immensely.

My two grown sons, Thomas Barry Brink and Eric Barry Brink, are a joy and inspiration to me – I love you both deeply.

I do have a critic voice that occasionally appears and I am most grateful to my dear friends Kathy Kennerley, Barbara Patterson and Lisa Senior for allowing me to have my feelings, being my cheerleaders when self-cheering eluded me and for lovingly helping me to get out of my own way. You rock!

I am grateful to Nancy Ruddle for your friendship and on-going encouragement – you knew there was something different coming in this chapter of my life.

Thank you to 2 of my sisters, Maureen (a.k.a. Judy) Sirois and Barbara (a.k.a "B") Westreich for your manuscript reading, re-reading, title suggestions and continued support.

Thank you Hannelore Goodwin, you listened to my heart and provided learning and growth opportunities for me, I am proud to call you my friend.

I spent many running miles discussing this topic over the years with Pat Glover and Judy Savage, thank you for your never-ending encouragement.

Thank you Janet Margusity, Gjoko Ruzio and Cyndy Webb for your love, support and (often unsolicited) on-going reality checks.

Lisa McMillen, thank you for exploring the unknown territory of book cover design with me and for creating wonderful sketches to bring creativity to the insides of the book. Genevieve Glassy of Gorham Printing, thank you for actually doing the cover and text design and for your inspiration. Thank you Margaret Diehl, for your editing help. Jim Joseph, I appreciate your candid manuscript feedback, which helped shape both the title and opening chapter. Thank you!

I thank all my friends and especially my Non-Book-Book-Club (NBBC) members: Marie Almeida, Annette Antolik, Marianne Cawley, Barbara Fitzgeorge, Sue Lambo, Mary Lee, Lisa McMillen, Jeannie Miranda, Barbara Patterson, Joanne Quinn and Lisa Senior, for sharing my happiness when I started this.

Lastly, I ask forgiveness of all those who have been with me over the years and whose names I have failed to mention.

It really does take a village and I'm glad you are all in mine!

ENDNOTES

[1] Dr. Emoto passed away in October of 2014. His work and pictures of the gorgeous snowflake-like crystals can be found on the website: http://www.masaru-emoto.net

The snowflake drawings in this section and at the end of the book were created by Lisa McMillen as a representation of the beautiful snowflake-like water crystals in our bodies resulting from the loving and kind words we speak, silently and aloud. It is not an actual snowflake crystal from Dr. Emoto's research. Lisa McMillen's amazing work can be seen on her website: http://www.cicalisadesigns.com

[2] Dr. Christian Northrup, MD, is a world-renowned women's health and wellness expert and best selling author. Her amazing words of wisdom can be found on her website: http://www.drnorthrup.com

[3] Neal Donaldson Walsch is the author of *Conversations With God*. His powerful book series shares his two-way communication with God. To learn more, please check his website: http://www.nealedonaldwalsch.com